The Unlimited Light of Creation

Revelations from Heaven

Natalie St. Tours

BALBOA.
PRESS
A DIVISION OF HAY HOUSE

Balboa Press books may be ordered through booksellers or by contacting:

Balboa Press
A Division of Hay House
1663 Liberty Drive
Bloomington, IN 47403
www.balboapress.com
1 (877) 407-4847

Because of the dynamic nature of the Internet, any web addresses or links contained in this book may have changed since publication and may no longer be valid. The views expressed in this work are solely those of the author and do not necessarily reflect the views of the publisher, and the publisher hereby disclaims any responsibility for them.

The author of this book does not dispense medical advice or prescribe the use of any technique as a form of treatment for physical, emotional, or medical problems without the advice of a physician, either directly or indirectly. The intent of the author is only to offer information of a general nature to help you in your quest for emotional and spiritual well-being. In the event you use any of the information in this book for yourself, which is your constitutional right, the author and the publisher assume no responsibility for your actions.

Any people depicted in stock imagery provided by Getty Images are models, and such images are being used for illustrative purposes only. Certain stock imagery © Getty Images.

Print information available on the last page.

ISBN: 978-1-9822-0933-9 (sc)
ISBN: 978-1-9822-0934-6 (hc)
ISBN: 978-1-9822-0935-3 (e)

Library of Congress Control Number: 2018908844

Balboa Press rev. date: 07/30/2018

Thank you, God, for your wisdom and knowledge.

Contents

Preface

In the middle of the night, God often wakes me to write. He calls between 2:00 and 4:00 a.m. There were nights I felt I would never sleep. He knew I would listen. I have always felt I should be writing. As a child, I would journal and write poetry and insights, thinking to myself, *we have so much to learn.* Writing seemed to come naturally to me.

As a young girl growing up in Amarillo, Texas, I would sit in church, listening to my grandfather's sermons. He was the epitome of a southern Baptist preacher, with the hellfire and brimstone approach. I sat in fear as his voice shook the sanctuary, slamming his fist down on the pulpit, wiping sweat from his brow with his handkerchief. I was afraid of who God appeared to me in the images my grandfather portrayed.

I wondered why I felt so bad about myself as I listened to the guilt and damnation roaring through the church. He spoke of going to hell if you were a sinner and said that we were all sinners. Rage seemed to be his verbal expression. There was no kindness or love involved in what I felt or heard there. If God was so good, why did I feel so bad? I never told anyone how hard it was for me to try and make sense of it all. Why would anyone want to listen to all the negativity?

What became the most impressionable view of myself: I was guilty as a sinner, I would always be a sinner, and I was unworthy to experience something better. I understand now how much this view influenced all my relationships in life, including that with myself. It was hard for me to love myself, to see something beyond the sinner complex.

Throughout my childhood, adolescence, and young adulthood, I always felt I was being watched. Yet, to the contrary, I also felt very alone. I didn't seem to fit in anywhere. I didn't understand religion. Until I was in my thirties, I could not even say the name *God*.

Growing up, I quietly questioned everything in my heart, wondering what life would be like if God really was loving and kind. I wondered how Jesus was our savior and what he was supposed to be saving us from. Even as an adult, I found it quite difficult to understand what I was hearing at different churches. The common names and concepts I would hear included God, Heaven, and Jesus. *What do they really mean?* This question never seemed answerable to me.

Insufficient data as to why I was here in this life kept coming up for me as well.

There was so much beauty in this life, yet everyone around me was in turmoil for one reason or another. Everyone seemed at war with their selves or each other. Even the people at church would easily condemn and criticize. I often wondered about the purpose and meaning of life.

At the end of my marriage, I began asking God and Jesus for help. I didn't know where I was going to live or how to support my three children. Right after that, a friend called me with a job lead. I was hired right away.

Soon after that, a member of my church opened her home to my three kids and myself until I could afford an apartment. All I had done was ask God and Jesus for help. It was incredible. We ended up having everything we needed. Everything was given easily. As a matter of fact, it came right to us.

When I realized how miraculous this was, I knew it had to be more than a coincidence. I had received everything I asked for. That got my attention.

In the dynamics of life, beyond the limited versions of possibilities that we see on the planet, I began asking God, Heaven, and Jesus for everything. My attention became focused on unlimited potential.

I recognized that the dynamics God was showing me were given with love. I learned on a deep level how important it is to know that God will offer all I need without condemnation.

Since then, I have become increasingly able to hear the voice of God. He sends Jesus to me, and I hear God's voice with Jesus. When Jesus comes, He often brings the company of angels, who offer guidance and support.

I have learned that God gave me inner consciousness that would connect with all life and that the heaven we seek *is* within us. There are dynamics beyond our comprehension occurring everywhere through all of life.

I was called to write essays for heaven that would encourage humanity to awaken and remember who they are. I am blessed. I am grateful for the longing to remember and know myself.

Many blessings with love,

Natalie

Live to be a part of your lives' consciousness as you master your years of evolution with heaven, healing each other and restoring Earth.

—God

Introduction

During the course of reading this book, one might choose to enlighten themselves. That is the finite infinite decision you will all make. Yet you are still living in human bodies, seeking outside your true selves.

The soul within this human body of Natalie, coauthor and writer of this book, *The Unlimited Light of Creation*, was once unknowing and yet sought to know herself. She recognized a deeper aspect of herself. It was difficult for her to understand why anyone would want to be here. Her soul began coaching her as she struggled to overcome barriers to happiness.

Her desire was greater than her sorrows. And so, she began asking God to help her. She didn't even know if He was real, yet she desired knowledge. When that desire became great, God opened doorways within her.

While she opens her heart, God reveals heaven's truths to support and reflect upon what Jesus shared with humanity throughout His life. He was an example of life, of God, and of the whole of love. He expressed great love for life, of which you are all a part of. Know that you will come to learn how important you are in the tapestry of life.

Listen and look without fear in your hearts. Listen to what

God is saying to *you* in your own lives while you contemplate His messages relayed here. The prayers of your heart will be known.

This is a connective, contemplative revelation that serves what humanity is collectively ready to learn. Your history does not include the whole story. Jesus is part of this life you live, and yet He is not called to serve you in shackles.

You are all eternal, as Jesus is. He is a master of light, living and embodying with you. You are all part of His collective body of light within heaven and earth. His body serves the earth as you serve the earth. The light serves and lives with you.

And so it is.

Amen.

CHAPTER 1

Mother Mary

Part I

In the beginning, God made life. There would be life throughout His union. And in this union, there would be order.

In this order, there would be cooperative energy beings. They were called forth into being so life could commune.

Divine law said, "Let there be diversity in creation." God then created extensions of Himself. Every extension of God exists within categories of the Law of Creation. Within the category of mother energy, a being called Mary came forth. It was God's joy to create Mary's divine resonance. And so we began a new chapter in life called the Divine Feminine Era.

This era has also been noted in many eras as the Holy Return. The master healer of Earth, the Dove of Jesus, carries Mother Mary's embodied life directives to the planet. His empowerments will always connect through Earth into your hearts and minds.

In this era, Mother Mary resides as His peace. Her divine energy signature of love greets humanity. She is a coordinate of light with heaven that is a part of every aspect of life. That which God provides through Mary, in Jesus—illuminates everything. Now is the day of being in the heart of Mary. Within that heart, remember that you are always with God.

In the peace you receive with Mary, a number of changes are set into motion. It is a time of change, corrections, divine unity, and love. Whether or not you understand it is unimportant. The activity of love is immoveable. When your heart understands there is no separation from heaven, communion with God occurs.

You begin this life wherever God sets you in motion. Throughout your lives, you will continually begin again and again as love. Everyone on Earth loves. You all desire love. It is part of your DNA, part of the genetic memories God gave you, created with the base power of love. Whether or not you feel the fullness of love or the peace it carries, it is still empowering your growth. Love empowers peace.

Mother Mary's base foundational directives serve to awaken peace within humanity. Her energies of peace, knowledge, hope, faith, and love are always streaming into Earth. Hers are the qualities of God as expressed by Jesus.

Peace within your being is a beautiful enrapturing. You begin in God's presence, breathing His love when He created you. And in His creations, you were all given the directions of divine life. You hold these directions as powers within your God created being. You are beings of soul, living in human bodies of flesh. These bodies require continual love and feeding of love. Without the energy of love, no one would thrive.

As you remember your importance in life, a new story begins. It threads your thoughts toward each other as you integrate into the awareness of God's love. When there is love pulsing in the world, a sense of unity and belonging occurs.

As love progresses in your awareness each day, your definitions of life shift to something irrevocably rich that sustains and supports you. Without the viability of love, many life changes would seem difficult. Love breaks through anything you could perceive as difficult. You will experience deep change at times.

You may not see the silver lining at first. Yet the best advice I can offer you is to be with love.

When life appears as difficult, know *what is real* will carry you. Asking to be fed by the divine energies of love is your divine inheritance. When you see with eyes of love, difficulty dissolves.

In your quest to remember love, life commands that you learn. To live intentionally with heaven commands that you are aware in life. Give your attention to heaven and earth. In the physical life, Jesus, God, and Mary merge in your spirit. The task of heaven is to support your innate knowing. As you embody God's attributes and as they come through you, new layers of awareness are revealed.

> *The empowerment of this lesson comes to encourage*
> *every thought toward God.*
>
> —*I AM Jesus*

When you seek love, look first within. And so, *in love*, you follow that which accompanies love.

It is the intention of heaven that you know who you are. You are meant to see beyond the limitations you experience in life.

The vast network of joy that comes through Mary delivers a sense of peace. Her love is gilded with God's peace. Her coalescence and qualities of being embody that which God is. Therefore, she is a deliverer of His being. There are no differences between who God and Mary are when she delivers Him. She and God are one.

In the great family of light on Earth, you live and give as you are given. The family of Earth resembles not what the truth is in full, yet you are a part of it. When the seeds of change awaken you into the collective embodiment of God, the threads of His being coordinate and occupy the symphony as one.

The value of family originates in heaven with the divine mother-father truth. The value of God is assembled into masculine and feminine qualities. They are part of a great dynamic in life. Every cell is part of the mother-father dynamic. Your mind is part of this function.

The origin of Mary is created in the wisdom of the divine mother and father. Her mission and directives for all life offers God's comfort, peace, love, and empowerment.

The doorways of heaven operate as love gates connecting you with God. In the presence of God, Mary resides. God brings Mary to you when life appears difficult. As you pray for peace, the wealth of love that carries it brings forth Mary's peace and love to carry you.

Her wisdom becomes your wisdom. Her peace is your peace. The feminine of God, as Mary, also shows up in you as loyalty. That loyalty is a guidepost for all life. It sees all life as important. It sees love in all creation. It gives the purity of love and peace to all life.

Purities of God called unto you creates a rhythm of knowing within. It is the contractions of birth that come when a woman has gestated to a ripening of her divine matrix. The aura of divine matrix you each carry within and around you is embedded with enumerable contexts of data directing, empowering, and exuding God's joy—the joy of divine motherhood.

In divine motherhood, Christ creates directions—as in that of a map. The ultimate goals of these directions are encoded in genetic connections within the aura's makeup. This is a simple composite of how light encompasses your body and directs information. Within your aura's template is a community of ideas, intentions, and pursuits, along with arrows to empower you toward a higher good that follows God's blueprint for you.

At times, God gives you direct knowledge through dreams. Know that, when this occurs, it is part of His appointed timeline for your personal growth. The divine anointing of God's consciousness directs you to listen to the ideas that form in your mind.

Be not uneasy if you do not understand your dreams or the messages in your mind. Pray that you will recognize and know God's guidance and that He will show you the way and direct you along your path.

Be not uneasy if you feel alone. It is you who ignites the fires when the darkness of doubt and unknowing comes over you. Peaceful accents of love always finds those who will God's help, illumination, and courage.

All prayers for help are always heard. The most important ingredients in healing have more to do with the intentions you create. Thoughts within you, examining what you think is occurring, can often detour your highest welfare. When you choose your highest welfare in your decision-making, let God choose what is in the highest and best good for you.

Be not dismayed at the time it takes to receive God's answers for you to achieve a goal. Life is unlimited. In human time, humanity suffers over the longing for immediate results. Unbeknownst, the creator has already examined each desire, each heartfelt longing, and every prayer. Every note of your soul has offered you many suggestions on how to do what is needed in order to remedy the way you feel, think, behave, and create.

As a human thinks, so he or she is; so he or she creates.

Every power God is *you are*. As infants in learning, I am here to clarify your opportunities for growth and for following your divine blueprints.

—I AM Mary

In the mother of all mothers, goddess of all gods, I created the giver of gifts. It was the temple of giving I created. In the creation of my kingdom, I gave admittance to my dream. It was the dream to bring alive connectivity. In the piece I created that I call Mother Mary, I admitted my wholeness to her. Therefore, she has and is my likeness. God, the omnipotence within her, resides as I AM resides in God.

—I AM

Part II

I am Mary, Mother of God Jesus. You may call Him Lord. You may call Him Jesus Christ. You may call Him what you will. Yet, God Almighty, created all God is. Jesus came into the Earth as my child. I nurtured and cared for him. I gave Him guidance. In His eden of life, the Christ of His being came to Him.

Hu, as in the *hu*man aspect of His being, is purposeful for His life. Hu is the Christ energy. Hu is the being. Christ I AM pressed toward His being and created the value, Jesus, Lord Consciousness. That consciousness is part of your lives. Humanity came into being with the presence of God in them.

As a being of light, I contact you in your dreams to help you remember the feeling of *Home*. Home is the place God made for you in your hearts where you are able to hear, know, see, feel, and be with Him—His love, His peace, and His wisdom. He is the key to your lives. He is the being you also call Jesus. He is the vehicle of light, omnipresent in all of life. Home is where you find God waiting to help you. Everything God made for you awaits you there.

In the gratitude for all life, Jesus begets the energy of the *Field of Being*. In the being of *All-Being*, God dwells. Stating, "I am grateful," manifests the words of wisdom that *God is*.

In the peace of God, the wisdom He created for you, connects. In the welfare of all life, the omnipotence of His being, codes you – authors of life, to embark your beings toward the magic that I AM continually gives you. Be that which God is. Be in your hearts. Be omnipotent in your thoughts, for they truly are *with* all life.

Quantum energy enfolds in a way that completes, honors, and directs the exact consciousness love intends. In this modality, the recipe of God's peace tools atone for the cooperation of humanity. The atonements support renewal and corrections. Coalescing into material life and attuning into terrestrial compositions, the purest and best energy of light comes into being.

> *Humanity is walking in God's kingdom in time to honor the truth of love and to be it.*
>
> —*I AM*

As God gave to humanity threads of divine direction and empowerment, heaven and earth would begin to evolve, moving forward as commitments to the *Second Amendment of Light*. It is the amendment that caused life opportunities; which led to inordained messages and direction of the fallen ones.

When the fallen ones chose against God's will, His love was such that, in the second amendment, He allowed for their return. He allowed for correction. He allowed the choice of love. And that is how the second amendment affected the union of all creation—the *Union of Love*.

Through the course of eternal life, God's master plan is to continually offer viable opportunities for renewals into the union of love. The fullness of this cohesive union has remembered for those outside love's cohesion.

In the first thought toward love, omnipotence renews and embodies all who would receive. In the peace and joy of love, remember that those who fell are still asleep in their own creations.

Intimacies of love will come back to humanity as you honor and call forth what God is. Deny unlove. Remember that masks of evil can seem true. Yet they will never begin in I AM.

In your name, as a soul, I have given I AM codes.
You, in my name, are the name truth. And you, in
the name of truth, can only come forward in my
design.

—*I AM Jesus Christ I AM*

I am the peace and presence of God as Mary. My job on Earth is to continue directing Almighty God's will in love, that His divine devotions have access into your hearts. My divine nature is true love in the being of all God is. In my codes of being, Christ and I direct heaven's powers. They are the archangels in the toolbox of your being. When you see them in your hearts, know they are here within you and that, you are a part of their illuminous life purpose.

As a family member of light, I am grateful in knowing peace. Almighty God gave us a witness for His family. He is omnipotent in Almighty God's kingdom.

Jesus came in His name. In His name He is written as Joshua Ben Joseph, who once lived through ten different galactic realities. The realities were made to help learn what I AM would provide for Earth. To be a lord for any planetary body, one would go to these realities for energy upgrading.

The upgrades would enhance Joshua Ben Joseph in His earthly reality. God made this compliance for all life, that you would all come to heaven and energize your beings. To access and energize within these realities, one must attend God's First Amendment in Light, "The will of God is my will." In that amendment and through your desire to abide in it, one will access many conversations with the lord of Earth.

In my code of being, I was given direct lineage through Jesus to attend in all upgrades in the heavenly realms. My greatest energy of love attained in those realms manifested God's innermost dialogue for nurturing the love for life.

Hu, as in your beings, will always want that nurturing of God in you. When you arrived into this Earth plane, the inanimate thought would not enter your thoughts. You were still within your master being of light. You were still conscious in that manner. You still remembered.

That is what God is impressing in your hearts now—that you are love. You are the best of love. You have and are immaculate love. Everyone you know has love in them. They are the beings God gave you to learn with. You learn together. You try and try and try. You do all you can to understand why you are here, why you were born, why everything occurs, and what you must learn at this point in your partnership with love.

When love calls to you, there are many connections of love energy flowing through you. In reality, your life is full of potential. When you guide yourself through love, these love energies coagulate to create the best formula for you.

You are all going through challenges. Do you not all remember the challenges of your youth? You were once pure at heart in your trust. As an infant, you know only love. The simplest dynamic God made for you was to be continually offered as love in the main vein of His consciousness.

As the child grows in his or her human expression, the love God innately designed to hold and energize this wondrous being would not be called innately. In the day of the fallen ones, humanity's genetic codes were altered. God's children became unable to hear Him and see His will.

His will is such that no evil can overcome the value of love.

In this message of loss, God designed a new amendment to repair and reenact his biocode formats. In the eons of Earth's history since then, the power of God has come into Earth, reformatting and correcting what was lost. New information in essence of love called *agape* would now be known. Your DNA profiles are now awakening to their new origin of light profiles.

When Jesus came, many who heard God and knew of Jesus, called the Essenes, were intuitively compassionate and willed that which God coordinated within them. They knew the pathways in this Earth that connected them. The value of this message came at a time when barbarism was occurring. The masks of many divisions called churches made no effort to know God, yet continually upheld what was unkind in life. They had no knowledge, yet claimed it.

The Essenes were in God's coalescence of being. And in His being, they knew the sacred activity. In each moment, the love they chose directed them toward momentous automatic culminations of truth within their tribe's collective heart.

The fallacies man made began and continued until the Fall of Venus. When I say this, I am remembering how much Venus did affect the direct energy factors of human evolution.

In the Milky Way, all planets direct energy. They are powers of God that He gave within the solar system. And so the beings within these planets were called into divine council with God. They were called to commune with God and interact through His being for humanity.

The prayers of many galactic beings commune with Earth continuously in order to aid, repair, and cocreate with the new divine master powers of God on Earth. These beings are emissaries of many complete beings who have evolved beyond Earth's realities. God guides them to greet and empower humanity with and through their knowledge of divine cooperation, divine love, and divine creation.

Through Venus's efforts, the will of God ended many catastrophic events for humanity. The energy of their intuitive, collective value is continually offering Mother Earth regenerative messages of hope. In the love of all God's witnesses throughout the Milky Way, Earth has begun to interact in my voices of nurturing life.

Love correlates within all aspects in the will and powers of creation. Within the codes of light, it is called *Agape for All Life*. The unconditionality of love for all life can always be in your thoughts, in your hearts, and in your decisions.

This is the path of the master in your being. He is lord of your Earth. And He knows what you desire in your life. The directive of His soul will ignite the power of your light to automate what you innately are.

Your soul has never been apart from love. It knows your desires as well. And in the path of your lifetimes, your soul directs ideas to its hu aspect.

Within your human aspect, you will always have God's conscious energy, which He made for you. And so you will continue to create new lifetimes in order to evolve into agape love for Earth.

Intimacy in life has been expressed through time as something shared by one lover with another. Yet this intimacy of real joy exists in your hearts as the vehicles of light you are. You are vehicles of light awaiting Christ's intercessories of oneness. The Oneness of Christ begets peace, wisdom, and love all at once.

Overwhelming gladness of this joy ignites a new relativity

within your being. It is the sequel of your soul being, the one who is called to ascend all illusion. It is the vehicle you exist in and learn in. To know the joy God is and to remember that you are His image welcomes more enlightenments.

Humility comes with just one name—the love I give with it. It treats all life with regard. It holds the highest for all life. In the peace of God it is humility to accept and appreciate what love offers.

I am Mary, and I greet you in the voice of *Love*. Amen.

—I AM Mary

CHAPTER 2

Glad Tidings

I am God Almighty. I witness for the God of Earth in the heart of Jesus. I do so in the will of His mind and the thoroughness of His mother light within. We are the creators of all life you know here. In this moment on Earth, you will all consider yourselves divine. Yet unknowingly you are limited in thought.

My divine heavenly family liberates your hearts in the tone of heaven. That tone connects every mind on Earth to serve in a universal format. Therefore, you are all living components in a collective union.

In the gratitude of all life, Jesus begets when and how you receive the multitudinous directions that flow forwardly into your thoughts. Know that the value of your mind expresses and creates with life omniscience.

The duality of being alive on Earth resembles more than just physicality. In the fluidness of your thoughts and coalescence of being with life omniscience, Jesus articulates all God's gratitudes that encourage, embody, and direct in the value of creation.

In my currents of life, gratitude belongs to all life. In the gratitude of my being, life conceives of itself with my mind. Therefore, you are still, and with me.

Prepare your thoughts as you encounter my service to you. In the mastery of your own life, you designed a message for your thoughts with me … one that would awaken you to mine.

We, in the heart of God, deliver that which is given to enable awakening thoughts designed for your life. We are His messengers in life. We are the Archangels of Heaven. We work in union with life on Earth. We awaken that which desires knowing. You are all awakened within various areas of your brains. We coordinate in the master codes of your body, that you would have new dendrite cognition. Your minds are weary and need assistance to awaken and learn.

In the master codes of life, Jesus walks into your thoughts, your mind, and day to day living, so that you will have form into your thoughts. The forming of new thought is key here.

Within your thoughts, the field of being aids and digests with you what God offers through Jesus. Deeply we seat the gratitude of God with you each day. Gratitude complies and arranges God's will, mastery and the fullness of your mind's timelines.

—Archangels

"I am grateful," you say, when you think of your life. "I am grateful to live and be embodied with life."

I am grateful. This is the key to your existence. When you embody God's gratitude, you seek and become the wholeness of God's creation. You plant seeds for creation. Gratitude is the seed that sends itself out to all energy in order to materialize and cooperate with all that God is.

I AM in gratitude with all life.

—*I AM God*

In my gratitude, I offer peace, hope, wisdom, humility, and grace. These are the aspects of love, divinely coordinated as life arranges and serves itself without limit. In this modality of being, the unlimited is arranged in gratitude. The fullness of life is in motion in gratitude.

In each lineage of heaven, my key of light omniscience repeats itself. There are no divisions between love and love. We share the simple energies of Christ. That is the I AM message for God Almighty that courses through all life.

The gratitude of any human being *gives* to your Earth families and their ancestor's lineages. This gratitude continues giving to the animals, elements, air, water, all creatures, all plants …and greater currents within Gaia's matrixes. Christ knowledge, as embedded throughout your divine matrix of Earth, entwines through all life as well. God willed that every gratitude be shared in the webs of light on Earth.

Worth has become a very important lesson for all life. Glad tidings, when offered through Gaia, embed themselves within God's worth. Purities direct the presence of love to exude the optimal collective values of worth.

Affirming, "I love God," immediately repairs unlove. Affirming, "I am happy," directs joy into the lifeline throughout Gaia. Intentions of joy always increase the higher prayers for those who unintentionally create outside God's processes.

Prayers multiplied throughout the unknown dimensions of heaven exemplify the gratitude that joy amplifies. Purities of heart deliver the highest influx of the *Christ Mind Truth*. Direct knowledge thus invites itself to all people on Earth.

Those who understand are those who take time to pray, meditate, and hear what feels right. This feeling nature, as noted in biblical scripts as a gift of the spirit, was embedded in each of you. No creation of God's will could ever be alone.

On the best days of your life, divine knowledge does appear to you. The presence of love completes ideas, sentences, and shows up in ways you could not have created on your own. The powers of love deny no one their grace. They offer the highest truth available that each of you are able to conceive at any given time.

Purity has also been thought of as a subject of cleanliness within. To "die of all sins" simply implies you are learning to overcome periods of unconscious, unknowing, egoic living. Decisions based on egoic creations, evil or *not of love* creations, means that you are simply denying yourself the God given and embedded powers you all are.

Praying for consciousness of love denotes nobility, humility, calmness, and security. Cleanliness of being is atonement for denying that which Christ has offered humanity throughout Earth's history.

The inheritance of Christ is atonement. That atonement aligns you with your divine heritage of divine mother love, which always knows and always forgives.

In that forgiveness, the divine feminine energies correct energetic patterns in your aura's matrix. Through honoring the Christ mind, I AM families of light cocreate new bountiful, powerful, and lovely new energies to clean your aura. When you pray in God's name of Jesus, your aura is amplified to accept the Law of God into your being.

God made us as beings of continual expansion, growth, learning, and cooperation in union. The divine matrixes of life within heaven, gives all we are to all that is within this cooperative empowered union.

Being awakened as a being of love implies you are trying to understand what you have collectively suppressed throughout history. Being awakened as a soul implies you have remembered that God is a creator, directing and choreographing His divine placements for all life.

Being atoned in gratitude implies that you acknowledge the past illusions that kept you in the darkness of unknowing. In the knowing consciousness of divine love, deep penetrating gratitude develops and multiplies in strength.

Families of light, do not dismay at the illusions you made. Do everything in your hearts and minds to feel my joy and soul love for you. Remember that purity is yours.

And so it is. Amen

CHAPTER 3

Christ Mastery

I am Jesus, God's son of light, given to oversee life on Earth. The revelations of the past can no longer be accessed as part of your new lineage. The story of humanity is evolving beyond the level of that knowledge.

It is time for the Earth, humanity, and all its elements to rise in light and consciousness, to overcome what has limited your minds.

Now, in the mastery of Christ awareness, I infiltrate your thoughts to anoint that which is good in you. The attributes of Christ consciousness evolves, empowers, and inspires humanity. It coordinates, derives, and lives as a body of light living as *one master*.

In the Christ mastery, methodically I account for every thought in your hearts. I account for the images in your mind, for your thoughts, and for your deeds.

In life, I will see each of you accomplish many tasks I appoint to you. When I appoint a task, God in me, codes His heart to life in order of code readiness. Deny not what you are ready for. Embrace the Christ knowledge you are given in thine eyes, within thine eyes.

Within my truest energy of divine knowledge, God's kingdom of joy, receives itself as humanity's collective joy. And within my

Christ knowledge, I AM governs my heart's joy and denies no one this joy.

In my peaceable activities, the icing on the cake is to understand who I AM is as each of you. Duality codes lie dormant within your heart's genetic material. My truth, intuitive knowledge, directs humanity's atonements of sins or errors. To error in life is a human choice. Yet it is evident an evil or something not of light codes encoded itself into all human DNA, RNA, and the codes of nature.

> *Duality has known itself through barbaric creations*
> *and yet strives to overcome them.*
>
> —*I AM Jesus*

Throughout history, humanity and the Earth have suffered. Divine intervention has eliminated many codes that are not of light or not of God. Now it is God's greatest will to uphold the Christ mastery for all humanity.

That which God made is to be known. To know thyself is to remember who you truly are in terms of the ultimate God-base knowledge. Let this knowledge be remembered, received, given, and lived. May it continually be a message of hope and healing for your lives.

Duality exemplifies the codes of light, which God made. Each of you are His God-based, light-based children. Do you not know what that means? When do you want to know? It is up to *you*. It *is* up to you. *When* is the question I offer you. When you read through my messages, give your heart permission to accept at least one idea. Allow your heart to remember what *does* resonate for you.

Love. Do you remember agape love? This love I speak of truly must speak to you. It is the base which you were created in. When you *know* God made you, you become aware of life differently. You begin to see things through God's eyes. In those eyes, you will find that God always invites truth at every opportunity.

When you look at yourself in the mirror, tell yourself, "I am a being of light. I am a being of joy. I am God's child. I am grateful to know who I am." Listen to your heart while the words are spoken. Listen to your own mind. Do you see how God works in you? There are times when you will listen and not understand. Try to understand that you have been asleep, living in an egoic dream.

This is the time for many of you, when the lessons of Christ appear. They are lessons in consciousness and they are lessons in heaven. The consciousness of light can reroute your mind's hippocampus activities, direct new dendrite connections, and encourage a whole new set of neuropathways to ignite the consciousness of light in the mind.

Within your dendrite connections, the neuropathways support a number of electrostatic energies. God creates these new pathways in order to upgrade your consciousness. Consciousness is thought within a collective formation of electromagnetic currents.

Within your brains are powerful webs of information. This is data you learned throughout life. In the consciousness of light, there are innumerable web portals throughout the known galaxy. Within this Milky Way web of light, God enters your consciousness. The consciousness He offers is one of love and kindness. The only exception is God's joy for life.

His love consciousness encompasses various qualities of being. Hope, joy, and peace are qualities of love. Agape love is the ultimate message you will ever receive in your incarnations as humanity. In His joy, you are accepted through His love. This is important to understand. Without love, there is no joy. When you fear something, can you even attest to feeling love, joy, hope, or faith?

There is something called adamantine particles of light that join you with God's conscious love. God did not make fear, only love energies. Within His love energies, Christ models His love to humanity through those who witness Him. They will see Him in the eyes of an infant. They will see Him in the eyes of innocence. They will see that He exists as everyone and everything God made. Fear has no rhythm of love within it. Therefore, it cannot be true.

In life, God offers thousands of opportunities to help you grow, learn, and understand who you are. The codes of light carry God's voice in every language. One day, you will all understand His whispers. One day, you will all know you are a being of light. And one day, the hope of God will have encompassed all of humanity's awareness.

This is the heaven I created on Earth. I am recreating everything continually. You, as in humanity, listen and learn. There is gratitude for all your efforts to align, to remember, and to coauthor with heaven. You will learn. You will know. You will come to a point that love can only revere in itself.

And so it is. Amen.

CHAPTER 4

Cohesive Light

I am the Christ, the Master God that made your solar bodies. Your auras are part of an eternal network through which the code languages of light flow. As a master in your own minds, the influx of data may one day be known.

In the light of day, your Earth revolves around a sphere so hot it can be seen by other galaxies.

As the *Christ Light of Day* encompasses the entire body of light, the unity felt within all, coalescences into this euphoric fellowship. It is the family of light you seek in your newly emerging awareness that flows in your bodies day to day.

In this witnessing of the Christ consciousness within humanity, you will see the value of humankind's collective thoughts harmonizing with the Earth. The Earth roots itself as an *Om* component. Om serves as equilibrium in your physical bodies, your auras, and your thoughts. It also serves as coordinates of energy called plasma conduits that interact in the planet's solar body, or aura, called Gaia.

This magnetic, galactic, conscious planet has within it everything God is. It expands in love. It expands God's love for you. It expands God's adamantine particles, which increase humanity's abilities to experience and express cooperative love.

In this cooperative community, love enfolds the entire planet's cohesive union. Every human being is included. In this miracle,

God inspires life. Know that you are important. God's recipe of life includes every miracle He created.

Through these miracles upon miracles, cohesive light expands energy. God's base foundation of light is agape. God made Mother Earth in agape-based light. Therefore, everything He made within Gaia is equally agape-based.

In the agape arena of living, the coordinates within you apply themselves within Gaia's matrix of life. The matrixes of all life were bred to coordinate and come together as one living family. Every aspect has an intricate component through which the Christ body of I AM consciously weaves its song for all life.

Within the *Song of Songs* and within the layers of life are codes of DNA called remembrance codes. They format your mind's awareness during new cycles in your Earth body. The fuel through which all life is carried, called I AM, blesses and nourishes your development through all lifetimes.

As the story evolves, the ever-expanding position of our creator in chief is that life know itself. And thus, all life will know itself. In the pleasure of all thought, the creator has evolved to listening and learning throughout all its aspects.

The master within each of you continuously relays information throughout the cosmos. This information coordinates with heaven. It notifies Lord Jesus when you are ready to move into a new segment of personal evolution. In each moment, I am observing and coordinating the next best position for your thoughts for integration to the holiest aspects you may observe.

Knowledge enables humanity to evolve. Everyone who appears on Earth, energetically expands evolution. Our energetic processes cannot be observed casually. Innately, you may understand the glimpse factor. It is simple and intuitive.

Families within families merge together throughout the cosmos, giving and receiving that which is expanding collective awareness. Earth is part of this co-axis of living, healed in the field of light that resembles the minds of its occupants. In the occupation of light, God's master coordinates for living coordinate the *breath of light*, which lives through all thought.

In the light that connects all thought, this Milky Way coordinates life on Earth. In the master plan of all life, you will see its reflections. Coded within DNA, RNA, and every atom is a Christ pattern. In the patterns of creation, every Christ similitude revolves around an inner core. This core neutron inhabits the Christ power of agape. In this dynamic of life you live, agape currents swell within the aura of all life.

Every living thing is encompassed in an aura of light. This energy breathes vitality of life in and through the human form. As in photosynthesis, a plant derives vital energy to transfer data in each cell. As within the human body, it too survives on a type of energy translation.

God made the planets to align in a unique energetic pattern. The patterns within this Milky Way express agape. They support dualities. They support continuity. They also support electromagnetic code energy translations.

All of this comes down to knowledge informing every area of agape-based life. Cohesive light comes within every minute particle in this Milky Way.

And the story goes eternally, throughout the collective fields of bodies called *coordinates of light*. They are all part of this soul within the master creator through which all life flows.

And so my life continually flows through the life of Jesus and flowing toward humanity. It flows through the continents, the blades of grass you walk on, the air you breathe, and the water you drink. The life you live is my life. It is part of my heart in the field of life.

—God I AM

I am grateful for this life with you God. And so it is. Amen.

—*Jesus*

CHAPTER 5

Duality

When I see my heart expand, peace comes.
                                    —I AM Jesus Christ

God hears everyone on Earth. Whether you know it or not, you are loved beyond measure. Everyone on Earth experiences the separation of being soul. You experience separation of spirit, your divine nature.

As a human being, you will learn to listen to and access the divine nature within you. Through your awareness is unique and countless combinations of thought called to your spirit. The duality of your mind knows not what the aspects are that correct it. The energy of the mind is diverse. Through diversities of light and Earth, a human being will access countless powers, ideas, and opportunities.

Thought represents connectivity in which currents of life participate. The male model coordinates many energies of thought, directing them to populate ideas. They are of the mental masculine energy. The feminine model within each one of you will access innate knowledge that serves love in the Earth.

As a being of light, you already know how the feminine and masculine energies coordinate with one another. As a human, the mind is often set up to only remember and coordinate with the masculine energy. It is God's will that Mother Mary continues integrating your hearts and minds with her sequences of mother consciousness.

The masculine has roots in conversation expression. It is important to know when communication goes awry, that the feminine has not been acknowledged. The feminine will always invite balance, order, love, fairness, equality, and peace to all discussions. When divine balance occurs, the diversity of life accesses the divine templates known as the *Hall of Records* or *Akash* in your auras.

This divine access acts as counsel for your thoughts, that you would enable your thoughts to adhere with the highest good for all. You are here to help harmonize life together. Imbalances are simply an opportunity to open the portal in your heart, your mind, and your soul mind to honor the very path you are here for.

Your divine lineage is that you be human and yet be soul. The divisions within your thoughts are counsel from different aspects of your mind. While a human being experiences the subtleties of heaven through soul, they also experience outward physical sensations and desires.

Within this duality format, heaven's doorways communes with humanity to orchestrate dualities that will balance. The mind can always access the features of thoughts that originated within God's mind.

The duality of being a soul in a human form will always comply with the Great Almighty. And through its impulses of identity the lower humanity experience either strives or struggles with this divine component. All around the globe, there are countless conversations either rooted in love, compassion, and humility or adversely in conflict, agitation, and anger.

The attributes of the heart, known also as the heart chakra, also longs for balance. It is the story of life that it resemble the image of life, which gave it life.

In the image of God, you associate with soul. In the physical reality, humans must grow into their divine heritage. When the template of *divine maturity* came into being, it was written that you would learn His peace, love, humility, unity, and wholeness.

In human lifetimes, there are cycles of remembering your divine heritage that, educate and support the knowledge needed for overcoming obstacles. When you have completed a cycle of learning, a new cycle begins. In the dynamics of learning, you will all come to know God is with you.

In the beginning, God examined His own being. What did He choose for himself?

> *In this unique question I remember calling myself twos. It was an idea of individual and separate realities within my own mind. And in my thoughts, a revelation occurred. I began questing within my mind, choosing, examining, and altering the acceptable parameters of what realities would begin and connect in my wholeness.*

> *In the duality of kindness, I designed a facet of kindness that would override what is and isn't acceptable in my wholeness. The soothing examples of my heart remembers how important it is to know thyself. In the codes I have written in your hearts are my everlasting truths.*

You will all come to know yourselves in time, in death, in rebirths, in time, in death, and continual cycles of the same, in order of alignment for your perfect evolution of growth. You will know yourselves and you will learn who you are in my image.

This aspect of my image has been proclaimed in a visual picture you see as human. Within the image of your minds, conceive of an idea uniting us in thought. And in that thought, you and I are one. We become unified into wholeness. That is where you will find me, in your heart's willingness to grow.

In the union of our oneness, I ignite the hu. As the image of soul, your light becomes integrated into mine. In the awareness of our union, you find yourself more aware of kindness, cooperation, and feelings of unity and peace. You find yourself looking at life differently, as if I were with you.

In this moment of knowing, you find yourself happy to know you are a reflection of divine living. You become more aware of God's will in this life. You become aware of your agreements in life with God and how important they are in your growth. In this activity of being, I reflect my consciousness as you, my divine creation.

Within every cell, thought, and breath is a design of union within the physical and nonphysical existence.

Your birthings in knowledge come in order of your readiness. The sequences within you—in your heart, mind, and body—already know the answers. You were written into genetic codes to adapt and learn. You will all come to know yourselves—however long it takes is your choice.

All humanity exists in my codes, which enlighten your minds while you live in humanity. While you walk the Earth, my codes are within you, and you enlighten all life. Life recodes itself while you do this.

—I AM God

In return, Mother Earth transmutes negativities, energizes them, and returns them to you as God's unconditional life force of love. Agape is the nature of God, and in that nature, God composes a symphony of living elements, events, decisions, memories, desires, and qualities empowering your minds. In this holy symphony, all life remembers, evolves, and cooperates.

I am the agape love you all seek. I am the Christ. I am Jesus. I am a being of God's will. I am His servant. As I serve, I give what God is in me. God gave me His infinite knowledge. I live God's love. I give it. I am it. I live the codes of light as He is. And so, my joy is to support all earthly agape-based life.

As a human, you want to know why I haven't come to you. I admit to you, I am with you.

You then ask, "Where are you? I do not see you. I do not know you. I do not understand. I haven't even come into a place in my life that would even support the idea of you."

I have always been in your hearts. I have always given people to you who would show you God's love. They were kind, peaceful, and loving. In the core of your being, you are kind, peaceful, and loving.

As God energy, you all greet God energy in life. Duality exposes each human to live and greet life just as I did, as Jesus. Do unto others as I am in my example to humanity. Give love. Give joy. Trust love. And remember that I came to show everyone you do not have to suffer. Love each other. Support one another and help each other. Do not argue. Do not worry. There are so many miracles waiting for you. Ask God, and He *will* give you what you need.

> *In the will of God, I give life to life. I give the*
> *love that God is to all life. My ingredients are to*
> *uphold His original agape powers throughout this*
> *Milky Way.*
>
> —*I AM Jesus*

Every human body contains an electrical aura. Think of yourselves as conduits that expose other conduits to information. Each of you are examples of Jesus. He is made in my image, and so are you. We are all conduits called *living light*. We emanate energy. We interact as energy conduits.

This agape energy within our auras contains my codes. We are all made in the same image. Do you not see that? As a human, you tend to judge each other based on differences. You must understand, God has given every one of you specific abilities. You express abilities such as being a good listener, being happy for others, and being supportive.

There are countless abilities I placed in your hearts. In your genetic codes, you each received directions. They are keys of life that define everything you are. Think of it as a map with conduits of data that shows what *you* were made to express and be, as a one of a kind, unique being in your God-given potential.

In the contents of love, you will all come to know and behave in my activities. When you activate the gifts I sew in your hearts, you remember what it is to exist in my knowledge, my life, and my heart. This design is made specific for your journeys as duality beings.

Historically, I have brought many to Earth, who I designed as engineers, storytellers, healers, visionaries, and those who would remember. I wrote a storyboard for every need. I detailed what life would be given.

When you look at humanity's histories, do you see the amazing and incredible beings you are? You are bountiful beings full of glory. You are resilient and always ready to learn.

I love you always. In life, you will know how much I do love you. You will understand the expressions love has given throughout many incarnations into your journeys. Do not worry if you remember not, that which is beautiful within you. The timing and peace within you has knowledge and will find you as sure as life itself.

I am in your hearts, and you are in mine. There are no ways you can separate us. There are only illusions in your minds to dissolve. In those illusionary times, give your hearts to mine. Be still and know I am with you. You will remember when you remember. Your heart already has the exact memory of my wholeness.

I AM God

Duality is about learning not what you came to look like, yet remembering what you are here to *be* as. You are more than appearances, more than money, and more than doubts. When you look at your limitations, remember it is the ego reminding you and it is the being within you facing it. There are no obstacles, only illusions of them. You are love transmuting ego's illusions.

Your destinies will call to you in many ways. Your hearts will desire more than what ego chooses. You will begin understanding more every time you aid your heart in gratitude, that God would guide you.

Within God's mind, you will all come to know beauty in your hearts. That beauty encompasses joy, peace, hope, faith, grace, and humility. As you connect in your hearts, you will understand there are no obstacles. In your minds, choose God in your moment of need.

Place your hand on your heart, thanking God for His help. You will receive it. You will feel peace and all it encompasses. He is more than you can ever imagine, and yet the main goal in your lifetimes is to know yourself. Be certain that God can and will override all obstacles, negativities, and illusions. You are the chooser within who chooses. Would thine will be your choice or would ego? Always ask God to dissolve ego.

Thank you, God, for dissolving ego. Thank you, God, for dissolving ego. Amen.

That is the prayer of prayers you will all remember. And so it is. You are here to learn. Peace be upon you. Love be upon you. Begin knowing that God willed you to be, and He willed you to learn. He willed you to accept that which is yours.

In your minds, I am yours. I am yours. I am yours, eternally. I AM is the being of light within all life, entering your hearts and entering your thoughts. In your minds, you must agree and *know* that it is so.

When you are free of ego, you will learn and know as you were in your wholeness. Being human is a joy. And yet it *is* a task. Learning about God and how He lives in you, adheres you to your wholeness, unifying your minds to Him, Earth, and unconditional love with each other.

And so it is. We are whole in our remembering.

God lives in and through everyone.
—*I AM Christ, I AM*

CHAPTER 6

Relationships

Deep within each person on Earth lies support beyond knowing. Intuitively, you each know you need one another. You understand that, whenever you work with another human being, you feel supported. As a human being, being given help is essential to your optimal growth in life.

The power of a relationship can be found in anything you see in pairs. The initial paradigm depicts a woman and man in an intimate relationship. You may even look at it as same-sex intimate relationships. However you interpret relationship, the intimacy and importance of the dynamics you experience either knowingly or unknowingly are all about the support and growth throughout all of life.

When a child is conceived, his or her intimate relationship is with the womb. There it receives nourishment to help it thrive and grow. Without this intimate relationship, no one could be birthed. It must occur. As life connects in your life, the ultimate awareness is that each of you will know what it means to remember how intrinsic all life is together.

Men and women are certainly viable components for reproduction in humanity. The tendencies of life itself will always follow the corrected version within its genetic profile. There are more opportunities to know why you choose variations in life.

Many individuals look within and notice they have an idea of who would improve their self-value. The tendency innately, is to seek what you need in order to grow. Intimacy within welcoming arms is always followed by a desire to connect and be filled again and again. Almost always, one or the other party in a relationship will choose to resist, in order to connect to a new pattern that provides greater growth. The tools you need to learn will find you as you trust the people you learn with.

While learning you each have something of value in life, you also learn there is something you each need to share together until you are complete with it. Remembering what you are here to do will not find you all at once. The infinite discoveries always try to offer many viewpoints to learning.

In beautiful atmospheres, one may discover something magical that happens within them. A drive within them opens somewhere undiscovered. And then it breathes something pleasing and nurturing within the eye of the beholder.

Energy exists in intimate relationships. It does and is evolving and moving as it listens to all of life. It is also encoded with its own pattern of knowledge in its own design to materialize itself.

In positions of men and women, there are countless opportunities to explore and grow. Intimately, they exchange ideas, affirmations, and rhythms of living. And so we continue the same interpretations within energy and how it moves and is directed by you.

In the time it takes to ask a question, you are already requesting an answer within. The intimacy of thoughts are quite empowering. The exchange is instantaneous. The ability to know things automatically is inherit in each of you. As a duality being, the Earth and all its creatures were encoded with the same patterns of living.

Empirically, the science of the ages has stumbled upon a frequency of events. Those events were about learning at a new level as to *how* you all impact life. The question forming at this point of view is, "How do I impact life?"

Intimately, you are communicating in Earth rhythms. This unity has been observed from afar throughout the ages. A beautiful example of this is that heaven now observes the initiates on Earth who affirm what they desire. When heaven hears anyone say, "Thank you. I am grateful and happy," they hear it as God's omnipotence calling all life.

No matter who you are, thousands upon thousands of thoughts are being heard by life in and through you at every moment. We are creating every moment, learning in every moment, and empowering life every moment.

In the circumference of life, agape love connects in all relationships. In the Christ mind, all life is interwoven as its ministry and talks in ways that may alter one's thoughts and ideas, connecting every human being to itself. Within life, God gives all of you *mastery codes*. Within the codes are relativity experiences. They enable each of you to accept ideas and reflect them.

The examples God gave in the lifetime of Jesus were about unconditional agape love. Now, within the codes of light, God enables humanity to accept everyone in the kindness of agape. Jesus gave multiple examples of agape. Being love is His first example, as a *being of love*.

In this beingness of His consciousness, Christ enabled Jesus to accept God's will of agape's unconditional love for all. Jesus willed to be in God's will, always. In His willingness, peace overruled any inclination of egoic thought.

When you enact the will of God, your relationship with

life accepts all love. Throughout eternity, the masters within heaven have each had to remember the example of God. In that example, each master thought of *why* it was to be. Why was it needed? Accepting love for all God made is a circle of agape love reflections. When you see love for one, you see it for yourself.

When you go within, you are accepting what God is within you. Within God is a number of cooperative heavenly beings, such as Jesus, the archangels, and all that God made within the ethers of heaven. In the face of many doorways within your being, the community of God's family is united through a series of unlimited omniscience in the consciousness of God.

When God is called, the whole of heaven replies.

—Agape

Truly God applauds all prayer, meditation, requests, and humble surrender. For when one human being asks one thing of God, a union of many will accept the request.

When I became enlightened in knowing who I was, the angels called to me and said, "Be not afraid of who you are." That was the best advice I had ever been given. No one on Earth ever told me what God had made me for. I continued learning when I prayed in solitude.

God inside me could even walk and talk with me. He showed me courage that would enable my examples to come. In all my examples, God always held my heart. He encouraged every word I spoke,

*every thought I had, and even the steps I would take
each day."*

—*I AM Jesus*

In the peace of God, your relationship to all things are opened
to receive the will and love God is. That is when you receive
miracles. When you access the beauty of God's peace, heaven and
Earth move and cooperate with His will. In the speed of light,
God can move agape love for all.

In Earth or Gaia, God made a template that said, "Let there
be free will." And so, God made free will so that humanity would
learn and remember His will and love found within all life.

In the unified, cooperative family called humanity, God
also enabled a cooperative consciousness. Every human thought
ripples throughout Gaia's being, interacting with all life on Earth.
There are moments in Earth's history when terrible changes
have occurred. When you experience devastating tidal waves,
earthquakes, flooding, and famine … it is in direct correlation to
what humanity has unknowingly created via God's cooperative
consciousness of humanity.

Sewn within the fabric of all life, God also enabled healing
templates for all His creations in Earth. When anyone prays on
behalf of all life in Earth, enormous ripples automatically override
enormous negativities.

You have all witnessed periodic moments in time when it
seems people everywhere are exchanging the same ideas in your
internet, on social media, and even in social circles. When you
notice these things, remember that you once prayed for that.

Everything you think, say, and do matters exponentially. Do
not discount your abilities. You were once shown within Jesus's

life that you would have gifts. The gifts of prayer and intention, in thought, and in word were all shown to you.

Sewn within the fabric of all life, you have all become a weave of many tapestries. Wars will be changed over time. Famines will be removed over time. Anything you design in your hearts that aligns with the will of God, will prevail. Do not doubt the relationship you are to all life. And remember, most importantly, that God will override intentions of evil.

In your relationship to all life, reevaluate who you are. Do you hope what God would hope? Do you ever want peace on Earth? Thank God for His peace in Earth and all life.

> *Thank you, God, for everlasting peace on Earth, everlasting love, and the will to always be your example.*
>
> —*I AM*

In your human condition, every thought toward one another relays itself into each other's auras. In human relationships, many unknowingly direct negative ideas toward each other.

Knowingly, however, one may direct ideas of love and peace and even healing. Everyone does this. Every human being has the ability to heal each other. Would you not choose to help one another? Would you not pray for those at war? Would you not intend the best for all? Would you not intend to love one another and forgive one another? And so, I say, *will* that all humanity participate in agape love for all life.

> *I am grateful. Thank you, God. Thank you, God. Thank you, God. Thank you for the abundant love*

and the abundant joy I am living in this moment. I am grateful for the undivided love amongst our Earth family. And so it is I abide in your heart and your will. Amen.

—Natalie St. Tours, author

CHAPTER 7

Oneness

God made the planets as a discussion over eons of time. The family of light that coordinates with God is a communion called *oneness*. In the oneness of God, a communion of peace occurs. Within this peace, light energies encourage the Om consciousness.

Om masters of the planets collaborate endlessly as unifying agents. They connect Om consciousness to all life. Om is written in the subscripts of life. Its origin is far greater than our galaxy. Subscripts within our galaxy serve as the memoirs of Om masters. Truly, the silver lining has come to learn about the Om masters.

The sublet formats are eagerly awaiting the arrival of the Om. It is the master's knowledge that serves itself throughout the ages, indeterminably connecting and accepting its omniscience. And so it continues that cycle.

In the format of Earth, the Om signature frequency is being heard, acknowledged, and enlivened by Earth, by elemental life, and by many of its occupants of humanity. The circle of life encompasses a vast Om network, communicating so eloquently that connections form just as new dendrites do for humans.

The symbolism of that parallel is part of a different dialogue. Yet there are energy formations already binding in your thoughts, ready to up-seed the energy and connect with it. The undivided aspect of all life has and always will be one body connected as one thought.

The one thought, as written in the diagrams of life, works in Hu and Om consciousness. In these diagrams, God willed cooperation within all codes. Angelic honors cooperate within the diagrams. In the mightiest codes of light, direct knowledge occurs. All the will of heaven is what God gave them.

In the coordinates of heaven for Earth, an unending stream of Om circulates, just as the blood of your human bodies. The articulate aspects move intricate webs of solitude known as *purity*. That purity value connects in your minds and souls so you would evolve, as Lord Jesus did and is.

In the oneness of all life, a strum or note filled with superimposed solitude is highly rich in adamantine particles. Those particles exist as building blocks for truth. As a master remembers, he or she may go within and learn that, all that God is will come forward in them and in their supports of Om.

When you support the Om structures, the quantum messages open up to you. They are awaiting your instructions of intention to create values resembling the creator. The Om simply requests your attendance. You mend your minds while seeing within the Om presence. Synchronistically, a vibration comes forward into your minds, where it dwells and serves.

The soul within you gladly aids your attendance there. Allowing the peace of this moment, fears and worries slip away. In a realm beyond the illusions, you find yourself floating as a molecule of light. Freedom becomes your identity. It is a peace beyond bliss. The enhancements of your thoughts that follow are remarkable, in that only love resides.

Seeing yourself beyond earthly worries, energy illuminates your pineal gland. Once the enrichments open the pineal, all the circuits in your aura and energy meridians quicken. The awakening in your aura invites the soul of the creator. When a body of beings unify in such a manner, it serves all life in the quickening and adherence of the *Laws of Light*.

In the sequence of events, a ripple of living light moves through the universe, offering what Om supplies. The enrichment of adamantine life works in this union to supply the wealth of God. That within God, continually offers the feeding of adamantine particles, allowing all life to continue living eternally.

All Om in adamantine particles exists in many dimensions of life. The third dimension on Earth exists with the lowest mastery of all adamantine consciousness. When the mind invites God in, intervals of adamantine are now able to be received. In that moment, all the honorings supplied through adamantine particles instantaneously uplifts your body and Earth life energetically.

Once again, instantaneous awakenings innately support the commandments of love on Earth:

Where there is peace in oneness;

Where there is joy in oneness;

Where there is hope in oneness;

Where there is *now*, the openness of oneness in each moment, the incandescence of your flame within energizes life around you and with the life Om carries. While the carrier of light encompasses life, and the company of all life oms as one… masters awaken.

When the mastery in *you* comes forward in the will to learn and learn well, the master will be complete.

And so it is. Amen.

CHAPTER 8

Glad Remembrances

All life God made was a symbol for His energy patterns. He made thoughts that created images. The images created more imagery, formatting new creation.

—I AM Jesus

The life I was given to live is His symbolism that teaches us love. I am the teacher and the giver love gives through me. My Lord status does appear in your symbolisms too. The value of each being on Earth walks in a way that resembles love.

You look to each other for love. You seek it in your own mind. In the consciousness beyond your abilities of knowing is a seed of thought. It wills to come to you. It ignites the starlight within you.

When the starlight ignites, God's will can be known. Knowing the value of your mind as that which lives in my mind, opens a doorway for dialogue. The thoughts I offer you resemble deep love, trust for yourself, trust for others, and faith.

For when the love I offer you is received, a ripple of kindness streams into your mind. It serves to support you in your own life, in your own development, and in the value you offer your new life.

While the thoughts of love support you, continue living.

Give your mind to your thoughts with me. Come to me at times of need. In clarity, you'll find I offer gratitude to help raise your mind's awareness. For when the thoughts of worry are revealed to deep gratitude, they dissolve.

One moment at a time, I give my proverbs in your heart. When I see where you are in readiness, the symbol of my heart will reveal the truth. You are a being full of acknowledgments awaiting your tongue. When the voice of your mind agrees with mine, the absolute revelation of truth comes.

"I know" is a Proverb. It does and is. All truth I relay with you is a counsel. It serves to help you remember, in gratitude.

I am the blessed ONE given to bless. That is the counsel for all. In my mind, I am part of God in the Soul of His Soul. We are connected together through my threads of divine being.

Creation is an ongoing master, remembering and remembering. To remember is to unify. The counsel we all see together is about cooperation as a divine body. The view within your thoughts will you to know something beyond the current knowledge you experience.

Feel that which I offer. Love that which I offer. And greet the seeds of confidence in love with your own thoughts.

See yourself as the blessed one. Know yourself as that. Know that for everyone. Know the value God gives you *is* your heritage.

To see and be with confidence, to love and give with confidence, and to see who light offers within you… held within my mind, delivers the utmost joy.

Love reveals itself. It gives unto its being. God is revealing that for you with your replies and requests. God will continue counseling all who come to Him.

In your hearts you begin. You look within for ways I offer

love through you. Think of them as opportunities to remember yourself and who you are with life. I give in this way. Hear your heart speak the sounds through your voice. Listen and feel. I am here. We are one.

- In the gratitude of love, I commune. I offer myself gratitude for life, that I am the life of gratitude.
- I am grateful to begin each day with a blessing. I am guided in love. My light expands and blesses life.
- I am grateful to be alive. The life God made me as has everything unique to my purposes. I love myself unconditionally. I am grateful I am me.
- I am grateful for the blessed healing occurring in my thoughts.
- I am grateful we are together now, that love walks with me and serves as me. Thanking life abundantly is my story.

The blessed events of gratitudes:

- When a server within you speaks aloud, listen to the energy of their thoughts. Listen to the feelings.
- *In gratitude* is the first part of their thoughts. All love initially speaks in gratitude.
- *I am grateful* is the infinite informer for life. Thine will carry the remembrances to us all.

As a speaker of light, one may choose to invoke a being within light's counsel. Mother-father are the counsels you inherently live in. They are called yin and yang on Earth. Divinely, they are actually conscious aspects with the divine mother and father who coordinate with you. Always you have them in your heart.

Attuning your thoughts to the mother-father frequencies attunes the Christ consciousness into your mind as well.

One aspect of the Christ remembers with you. Jesus was given opportunities to learn in His human experiences. He understands the way a mind is oriented away from love at times. He walked in the garden of evil as a metaphor of living outside love.

Where there was doubt, the feeling of not knowing arose in Jesus. It was His to know and learn. He knows your hearts. He knows your experiences not only in thought. He sees them. He knows when and how to support you and show you what is true.

—I AM

You will continue throughout your life learning and remembering. The day I remembered to speak in God's tongue, forever united me again as a soul in the body of God. I serve in this life, living and breathing, as a current filling each vessel with love and knowledge— created to restore the will and love for all life.

Destinies awaken in the breath of light. Dreams come alive, and unlimited potentials arrive in your thoughts. God wills the best for your hearts. You have unlimited access and invokings to create.

Bearing the messages of light are the paths of each of you. For in my name, Jesus, are the currents of *divine remembrances*. They serve all life. You are my blessed ones, who are here to help Earth live in its greatest story.

Allow the best in you to come alive. And so it is. Amen. I AM Jesus, Lord of Earth.

CHAPTER 9

Elements

Cooperating in Mother Earth requires conversations in her mind. When you cooperate with Mother Earth, the elements already know what you need. All that God is resides within them and *knows*. The divinity God gave them and dressed them in will always cooperate, as I AM does in humanity. In the celestial kingdoms, God Almighty created all life in His image. Where there is likeness, like qualities exist.

> *As I AM gives, all give.*
> —*God Almighty*

In the giving kingdoms of light, *we are one*. We are undivided as we come together in this union of oneness.

> *We are the kingdom of elements God made for humanity in the Earth. We support the greatest cause of light: The wisdom, the wholeness, the expansive experiences, the experiences of God, and the energies of ALL LOVE.*
> —*The Kingdom of Elements*

In the elemental kingdoms, we are many. We are sylphs, elementals of the air. In the air, we see codes of energy, the energy

God gives to Earth. Walking outside, take deep breaths …breathe the energy codes. Breathe that which God gives to you. And breathe the wholeness.

In the rainfall, every energy code is expelled into water. This energy runs through your bodies of water. When you drink of the water, pay attention to it. Give it gratitude. It has come through miles and miles to find you. Every sip has a gift for you. Know that wherever the gift of the water leads you, God is placing His imprint. Say thank you to His imprint.

> *The energies, the wholeness, and gratitude were all*
> *made in and through God's will.*
>
> *—I AM*

Being *one* with God and being *one* with Earth is the job of every element. Every element is a cooperating energy being. The elements communicate in the heavens and the Earth. Within this exceptional dynamic, a systemic whole being resides. That whole being is all life on Earth. In *you*, whoever reads this story, is a being so much greater and so much more than you have known.

You are one of the elements God made for Earth. You are one of the greatest expanses of God. You hold keys in knowledge. They are embedded in your aura. They accept and return love to all life. They are the conduits God made in your union called humanity.

In your elements of Earth and your conduits of light, a systemic creation occurred. This whole body of Mother Earth resides within God's kingdom. It is *your* kingdom as well. The energy of Christ dwells in your aura. The image and likeness of God are within that energy. They are the omnipotence in I AM.

As elements of light, humanity still has much to learn. They have not remembered who they are, and they call to us daily. In the day of light, meaning the kingdoms of light, order resides. Within this order of light, the I AM Order, Jesus, and His angel leagues are sent and given as gifts to Earth. In the orders of humanity, the will of God is that you would know thyself.

—*The Union of God and Earth*

In humanity's Earth body dwells the systemic modalities of rocks. In the rock kingdoms, the solace you seek is within them. They all have knowledge. They all have conscious awareness. As you contemplate that, remember all life God made has consciousness. And so the rocks repeat daily, "We are grateful. Remove your wars. Live in love. Give your heart to love. And love your heart." That is the best advice!

And so the orders begin in hierarchies. In Earth, the hierarchies are based upon expansive knowledge. That with the least and that with the most. It is as it is. There are no greater or lesser. There are only degrees of expansive knowledge.

When you look at yourselves, you see a minimal amount of cohesion to this family on Earth. Where the rocks are, listen. Place your attention in gratitude for them. They will come to your aid. All elements of life adhere to the God agape energies. Adamantine particles recharge them and nourish them.

*I am grateful for the blessed events of this moment.
I am grateful for the Earth and all its elements. I
am grateful.*

—I AM I AM `

*When the fullness of life extends itself, the power of
God and Earth collide.*

—I AM Jesus

In peace, love, and coherence, remember that all life around you is with you. They are part of the energies of light manifested to live with you and nourish you. Honor your families on this grand Earth of yours. You are blessed, and so are they!

Om. And so it is. The Elemental Kingdom with God Almighty

CHAPTER 10

Peace

We live on Earth as a unified vessel that would come together joyfully through the peace that God is. As a body of God, the streams through which your divine inheritance flows, comes peace. That peace delivers more to your soul and mind that you cannot understand until you ask God, in your mind, for truth.

The consciousness of life—flowing through I AM Almighty, through particulate matter, through the hemisphere, and into the Earth plane—comes into your thoughts as you sleep. Throughout your existence, you have been slumbering without knowledge.

In the thoughts of your awakenings, simply see them as your first glimpses while you stretch and yawn, for the sleep has been deep. Your minds will to know what you are here to do.

In the passages of this moment in time, your awakenings create a rhythm of balance, harmony, peace, and joy. They come as a package, for to delight in love is to delight in joy. That love and joy will always accompany the master seed for Earth.

Peace is that directive for the planet for which all blossoms radiate and flow. The seeds are adamantine messages, signaled to commune in your minds. And so, "Good morning," you say as you awaken, greeting that which is joy, unlimited in love, and full in peace.

In gratitude, we in heaven say, "Good morning life!" In that moment, life greets itself with love, enabling peace. It is a rhythm of life eternal. Flow with the life you are. Conceal not the best in love.

This peace you seek in your life exists all around you, in you, and with you. This flowing message of peace says, "God, I am with you. Life, I am with you. I am your eternal mind of light, and I am with you."

When your earthly lives are over, you will remember that we came as a body of light beings who would wear earthly bodies to help restore peace. We are all seeds of peace. I am the instrument through which it flows.

All life reverberates that message of love, *"Peace is here"*. *"I AM PEACE"* is the affirmation. I speak your hearts. When you speak this for yourself, I flow with you. We are together as peace.

As a soul, I embody the gratitude of peace. My gratitude expands you. Your gratitude amplifies my joy for you. Your mind delivers adamantine messages as well.

Through all your lifetimes, I have come to you, whispering God's love to you. His peace accompanies every message.

Know that the passages of your lives has been part of a manuscript for living. It is a living manuscript through which matter moves and life can renew itself.

It is my gift that you awaken to your heart's energy and peace. Enable that which is real. Live the power of peace in your heart. Live it in your thoughts. Show yourself love. Know the peace that you are *is* who you are.

Welcome your mind to acknowledge that you are peace. You are love. And you are my whole family through which I give and live in. My peace lives with you.

I am the creator in your directives for life. Live in your directives of peace. See your lives in the important role of offering love through my eyes. The gentleness of my heart will open each heart in your heart's path.

Allow my love to support you and show you divine peace written for life, that it will always correct and support itself.

Deliver my truth in your heart, for the seeds of peace will move all obstacles. Rely on my divine power. You are a vessel created to receive and relay the values of my being.

I am Jesus, your loyal cocreator in life. Do you not know that? Will you see yourself there? Do you will to love as I love?

Ask and know. I am here in your heart. I am always with you. And so it is. Amen.

CHAPTER 11

Consciousness

In the omniverse of heaven, directives of light connect. The wholeness of light directs itself in and through every universe in the energy of Christ. The imagery of light infuses information that is my will.

In the union of all heavens, the Christ masters come to each other to remember and examine when they came to Earth, why they came, and when they will return.

As the Holy Spirit in God designed, peace would be enabled through a vast network of His kingdom. He would integrate His will, peace, and love within your hearts. The divinities of all light come within His integrations of heaven.

In the understandings of heaven, you might consider possibilities, that you have many electromagnetic energetics in Earth, some of which are man-made. The cellular devices you carry exhibit a kind of energy transport. They pick up a signal, and in that signal, whatever energy it carries, connects with your device. You then dial a number on the device. The frequency of your device connects with the frequency of another device.

Each being God made is frequency.
—God Consciousness

You all carry a unique energy signature similar to that of a cellular phone. Conference calls also happen in your reality. When God sends out a conference call to Earth, He is signaling to all life simultaneously. Within every frequency of life, God encoded a specific frequency that is equal within every frequency.

I am coded to receive God's messages.
—Natalie St. Tours, author

In the collective stream of consciousness, electrostatic and ionic components or neuropathways of light integrate and culminate communities across the unions. Each union within each galaxy distributes intergalactic messages in the neurostream pathways.

All consciousness gives, flows, directs, integrates, influences, and manifests with God. Learning about your inheritance as a being of light ascertains the mobility of your own dynamics.

In the dynamics of light, God created vacuums throughout His vast kingdom of being. Each vacuum helps maneuver every thought that God is toward your thoughts, toward life in each planet, and toward outer solar bodies.

The influence of God is great. Sew within your heart the truth about your own being that manifests, integrates, and directs consciousness just as God does. Allow the thoughts of your inner being to offer itself the truth of love, hope, inspiration, devotion, energy of light and the energy of joy.

When you adopt the truth for yourself, love will offer greater truths. Allow this passage to roll within your thoughts. One thought can grow beyond into a reality of new ideas, whereas light can enable more enlightenments.

As the soul advances through each lifetime in knowledge,

love catapults the powers of God into view. Automatic knowing unfolds itself. Automatic writing, hearing, and energetics within your thoughts vibrate on a higher frequency and more often.

When you notice a thought come into your heart, remember that it too has traveled far to reach you. And yet there is only one thought of the divine master for you: *Love your heart. Love each other.*

The singular, most incredible event of your whole lifetime chorus is to evolve into the reality of God *in* you. The life you are has everything *in it*, awaiting arrival in awareness.

I am grateful. I am grateful. Amen.

CHAPTER 12

Grace

In the grace of God, my will is done. And in that grace, sweet, sweet love agape manicures the rays of peace. Within the peace that comes with love, peace examines only love. Within love, peace examines only peace. We are knowing beings who articulate also in love. Therefore, there is nowhere that love cannot exist. We are the workers of light in the omniscience of YHWH, keepers of all light.

—I AM YHWH

We are the grace of God. Peace is within us. Servers of all light, omniscient beings of all love, remember their own messages within the co-accessible universe called YHWH (Yahweh). Sew within your hearts the peace God made us in. We are here in your hearts.

We are serving God's peace within your hearts. You are remembering God's peace in your minds. Peace connects in all life. Love will enfold what God lives as in all life. Earth remembers the breath of life God gave it. Each exhalation reverses evil. Each inhalation inverses what love is.

Minds of light, codes of beings, creators of all light—follow your hearts. Listen to what love made. Remember that you are within that creation. Creators create what God made—love.

When the minds of light connect in your hearts, you are in community within God. Wherever this community of God resides—it is cooperating, offering love, connecting in peace, and lives eternal.

Magic materializes everywhere on Earth. It is found within the life you see and in all of nature. Listen and know. We are the *keepers of love*. YHWH made us in His image. We are Gods. We are unlimited. We are peace. We are love. True love comes from within. You are the makers of that love in the kingdom with YHWH, in YHWH. He is a *maker creator*. That makes Him the MASTER POWER of GOD. When you see these capitalizations, automatically understand the authority in the hierarchy of YHWH

Listen in your heart and know that Lord Jesus is within Him. He is a master within YHWH. As a peacemaker exhibiting God's will that, life be at peace—results in what it is to be a master, opening the pineal gland. Once open, you exhibit more remembrances and truths energetically, magnetically, and kinetically. The particles of your being exude through life. You all create as such. This is the *creator's way*. Know that you are the creator within, working in your own magic.

When the will of God co-unifies *as* your mind, God's peace automatically generates the will to commune with all life, preparing you and giving you what love is. God's peace illumines the way in your mind.

When the will and the co-activity of light coincide as one thought in your mind's eye, your pineal gland absorbs gratitude and love energy. This exudes what love is into the union of your being. When life exudes such love, you become one with all life.

While peace connects in you, histories of violence dissolve.

Know you are an important aspect of life healing life. God continuously upgrades the codes of consciousness for the evolution of Earth. In and through you, this consciousness ignites and energizes life.

Love created the pathways through which creation occurs. You are one pathway as a whole called humanity. Individually, microbially and ethereally, God created many pathways. As such, these pathways are the doorways of light. We call them pathways, as they reveal knowledge. They commune together with all life.

Through this communion, the transference of knowledge awakens life, breathes in it, and lives as it. There are no doorways of light you will not know.

You will evolve throughout your existence individually as a being of light. The purpose of your physical incarnations has been to experience enlightenment in knowing YHWH. He is the master of your mind's eye.

In the pineal of your mind, the chrysalis of life expands while you live. There are some who will expand and evolve more readily. They are accepting what God is giving them.

When you know YHWH has breathed in you, the pineal gland expands. The pineal listens and knows. It sees. It messages life. It telepathically orchestrates what YHWH gives to life through you. You are the automated messengers of love.

> *As my messengers of light, I anoint humanity to ignite and create with me. My pathway of I AM is the carrier wave of light through which all communion exists. Therefore, we are whole.*
>
> *—I AM YHWH*

> *We, the keepers of light, work with all humanity in*
> *Earth. We aid and support life. Jesus oversees our*
> *service through YHWH.*
>
> —*Archangels of Heaven*

In heaven on earth, you live within the realm of God's grace. You are the inherent keepers of grace that are here to embody the will and peace of light omniscience. By that will, love commanded to command only love.

In your minds, you are the keepers to live His will in thine will—in the Directives of Light and wholeness of all unity. And so it is.

Amen.

About the Author

Natalie St. Tours is a spiritual writer with God. Her years of devotion in seeking to know God's wisdom and her reason for being, created a commentary with Heaven. She now brings revelations about life, love, and autonomy that express our divine nature and heritage.

Made in the USA
Middletown, DE
23 April 2020